8 Pillars for Exponential Business Growth

8 Pillars for Exponential Business Growth

A Practical Guide to Building Your Bookkeeping Business

JEFF BORSCHOWA

authorHOUSE®

AuthorHouse™ LLC
1663 Liberty Drive
Bloomington, IN 47403
www.authorhouse.com
Phone: 1-800-839-8640

© 2014 Jeff Borschowa. All rights reserved.

No part of this book may be reproduced, stored in a retrieval system, or transmitted by any means without the written permission of the author.

Published by AuthorHouse 09/03/2014

ISBN: 978-1-4969-3732-2 (sc)
ISBN: 978-1-4969-3733-9 (e)

Library of Congress Control Number: 2014915510

Any people depicted in stock imagery provided by Thinkstock are models, and such images are being used for illustrative purposes only.
Certain stock imagery © Thinkstock.

This book is printed on acid-free paper.

Because of the dynamic nature of the Internet, any web addresses or links contained in this book may have changed since publication and may no longer be valid. The views expressed in this work are solely those of the author and do not necessarily reflect the views of the publisher, and the publisher hereby disclaims any responsibility for them.

To my loving wife, Shannon, and our two wonderful boys, Malcolm and Nathaniel. Your unquestioning support and love have made this book possible. I truly could not have written this book without you!

Contents

Acknowledgments ix
Caveat xi
Introduction xiii

Pillar 1: Operational Efficiency 1
Pillar 2: Marketing and Networking 23
Pillar 3: Sales 30
Pillar 4: Niche Development 34
Pillar 5: Value Pricing 39
Pillar 6: Technology 43
Pillar 7: Value Added Services 57
Pillar 8: Practice Management 62
Conclusion 74

Appendix 1: Bookkeeping Business Assessment Tool 77
Appendix 2: Leveraging the Cloud 79
Appendix 3: Recommended Reading 82
Appendix 4: 24 Secret Technology Solutions for Business
    Dominance 83
Appendix 5: Niche Development Example. 87
Appendix 6: Business Growth Experiment 93
About the Author 95
About the Book 97

Acknowledgments

Sir Isaac Newton made a profound statement: "If I have seen further it is by standing on the shoulders of giants." I would like to echo that sentiment, as I have been extremely fortunate to know and learn from some great thought leaders, both in the accounting industry and beyond.

There are so many people I would like to acknowledge. In the interest of brevity, I will focus on the people who led to the creation of this specific book. I would like to acknowledge the numerous people who have helped me throughout my career, including educators, mentors, clients, and colleagues. I owe all of you a tremendous debt for allowing me to learn from you.

The seeds of the path that led directly to this book were sewn at a chance encounter at a conference in Orlando in 2010. I met Rick Solomon in the hallway between events, and we began a dialog that would extend into the roots of this book. Rick encouraged me to seek my own truth and to find my purpose in serving others. Over the years, Rick and I have had many conversations, and I am honored to count him among my friends. Rick is too modest to accept credit for the achievements of the people he mentors, but I assure you he helped me find the path by looking within.

The next acknowledgment is for David Merritt, the creator of Client Track. David reached out to me, a complete stranger at the time, and offered to support my first cross-Canada tour to highlight innovation and technology that would help bookkeepers and accountants with building their businesses. We were overwhelmed by the positive response to our tour—we had clearly found a demand for information. The tour led to this book, as a response to the common questions that we received from participants during and after the tour. David is a true innovator, and I value his input into my processes.

Finally, I must acknowledge John Leishman of the Tursa Group. He is a truly brilliant businessperson, and his innovative approach to technology has helped me immensely with this material and with the book itself. I can say that John has challenged my comfort zone and pushed me into new areas of research and technology solutions.

Caveat

This is a summary of products and services that I have integrated in my practice, have used for my clients, or am in the process of evaluating. I will share my experiences, including challenges and opportunities. I make no guarantees that you will see the same results.

I urge you to visit the websites included in these materials in order to conduct your own research. This book is simply meant to provide a starting point and research options as you discover the power of the cloud and the paperless office.

I spent years trying to fit the traditional accounting firm model, but the concept did not suit me. I was turning away consulting work that I would have enjoyed because I was too busy with compliance work. This book represents my discoveries on the path to exponential growth.

To get on the right path, I had to question all assumptions about what I "knew" about running an accounting practice. I leveraged materials gleaned from conferences and collaboration with my peers in order to implement best practices and build my Dream Practice.

Introduction

Welcome. Since you are reading this book, I am going to assume that you are looking to build or remodel your bookkeeping business. The content you will find applies whether you are just starting out or you have been in business for years and want to take your bookkeeping business to the next level. Read this book as a guide in your quest to identify, evaluate, and implement new solutions for your bookkeeping business.

I have been in the accounting industry since 1991, and I have seen a variety of accounting and bookkeeping firms from the inside. The management techniques and tools varied, but ultimately most accounting professionals were looking to grow by implementing technology or expanding services.

What I found most unusual was the seemingly random results. Very intelligent people were, in essence, fumbling in the dark and hoping to achieve a better outcome by doing the same things, year after year. Albert Einstein defined *insanity* as doing the same thing over and over again and expecting different results. How many of us have met this definition of insanity in managing our business at some point or another?

Throughout this book, we will talk a lot about time and relationships. Specifically, we will examine the following:

- ways to save time in a modern bookkeeping business
- innovation and technology that have the potential to revolutionize the current bookkeeping business model

- new ways to think about the modern bookkeeping business
- expanding service offerings to increase profits and enhance client relationships
- emerging issues impacting the bookkeeping business

I started my own firm in 2008 with great intentions and a promise to myself that I would do things differently. I will admit that I spent my first year dealing with the tyranny of the urgent. I actually referred to myself as a firefighter rather than an accountant, as it seemed that all I did was fight fires. I was letting my clients manage my firm and me. After a year in practice, I decided that this was not what I had intended for my firm, so I made some drastic decisions and took a hard look at where I was with it. I no longer enjoyed going to work in the morning, and I was at risk for burning out. I had to learn lessons and make changes quickly if my accounting business was to survive the rapid growth that we were undergoing. In hindsight, I see that our rapid growth was literally a crushing success—I was being crushed beneath the weight of my firm.

I did not become wiser overnight. I invested heavily in attending conferences and courses in order to learn more about how to run an accounting firm. I was actually frustrated, as most local professional development offerings focused on the technical skills rather than the softer management skills needed to become a full-fledged entrepreneur. I began to travel to the United States in order to attend conferences. Those trips made the biggest impact on me personally and on my firm. I met inspirational people and learned that business problems are business problems, regardless of where you live or the industry you are in. Some of the courses I took were immediately relevant; others set me on a path that would eventually lead to change.

I dare say that my openness to change and willingness to explore possibilities have made all of the difference. I learned about innovation, product mix, pricing, and business philosophy from very bright individuals. I can say that many of my mentors have become friends, and we continue to learn from one another.

Through this journey of discovery, I came to realize that I personally love to teach and educate others. Initially, I focused on building my own accounting practice and helping my current clients to build solid foundations for their businesses. I knew that I was on the right path once I saw I had ideas that could improve the lives of my clients and that my clients were willing to pay me significantly more for the guidance I could provide. I then started working with bookkeepers and accountants as my new client base—helping them to improve their practices. I have truly built a niche advisory business, and I would not have it any other way.

My intention for you, the reader, is that you will find something interesting within these pages that resonates with you to the extent that it will guide you in pursuit of a more profitable and enjoyable bookkeeping business.

I encourage you to personalize your journey through this book by taking a moment to study the table of contents and determine which areas in your practice are causing you the most pain. Appendix 1, the "Bookkeeping Business Assessment Tool," may offer you deeper insight, and it offers starting points. Focus on the areas where you most need to improve first, but work your way through the entire book. I will share my thoughts and ideas that I have implemented either in my own accounting practice or in my bookkeeper and accountant clients' practices.

Throughout this book, I will refer to bookkeepers and accountants by the generic term *accounting professional*. In addition, I will refer to either bookkeeping businesses or accounting practices as a nod to popular convention. However, make no mistake; I firmly believe that we could be talking about any business in this book. Business problems apply to all types of businesses; only the examples change. Thus, do not dismiss a topic or idea simply because I use an accounting practice as an example, the examples are relevant for bookkeepers as well. While I acknowledge that some people feel accounting is a calling or higher purpose, I believe that we all need to consider the world of bookkeeping and accounting as a business if we are to succeed. Being successful in our business is part of a higher calling, for if we succeed, we may continue to exist to help our clients succeed.

This book is broken down based on what I consider the 8 Pillars for Exponential Business Growth:

1. operational efficiency
2. marketing and networking
3. sales
4. niche development
5. value pricing
6. technology
7. value added services
8. practice management

You may already have a successful and well-developed bookkeeping business. My intent is to write not about starting a business but about how to take your existing business to the next level. However, you can implement the solutions herein even if you are a start-up, building good habits and best practices into your business as you grow it.

One word of caution: take small incremental steps. Do not attempt to change all aspects of your business at once.

I will mention specific products or services in this book. These are provided by companies that I know firsthand. I either have worked with them myself or have worked to help my bookkeeping clients implement them. I will endeavor to provide alternatives where possible in order to facilitate further research on your part. My choices were made based on the best fit for specific circumstances. Let your own specific needs guide your choice of solutions and the priority of implementing the solutions you choose to grow your bookkeeping business.

Pillar 1: Operational Efficiency

Inefficiency strangles growth. If your business design has flaws, rapid growth will quickly identify them for you. The flaws usually appear as pain points—they quickly become the things that wake you up at night. In this Pillar, we will focus on the following:

- digitization of data
- project management
- work flow automation
- staffing alternatives

By first focusing on operational efficiency, we can build our businesses on a solid foundation.

Digitization of Data

As a bookkeeper, you can take a quantum leap in your efficiency if you embrace digitization of your data. First, I will discuss how a bookkeeping business can enter the digital age. Then I will finish this Pillar by demonstrating how you can help your clients go digital as well, realizing further gains in efficiency and creating a new product offering for you.

If yours is like most businesses, you are in one way or another struggling with your paper. Digitizing your data can improve operations significantly. I have worked with several firms as they transitioned to a paperless environment. The process can be daunting if you do not have the necessary skills or expertise to do this with your existing staff. I have also seen a few mistakes made in the process, due mainly to lack of experience with the process.

I personally recommend that my clients seek expert help with going paperless, as it can significantly improve results and expedite the process. I have worked with Tursa Group (www.tursagroup.com) with my current clients. They offer a five-step process and a project management team member to facilitate your paperless project. Their five-step process includes the following:

1. digitize your data
2. document systems and processes
3. implement cloud-based services
4. outsource tasks to improve efficiency and flexibility
5. embrace telecommuting as a strategic initiative

I will examine each of these in further detail.

1. Digitize Your Data

- Go paperless. The easiest way to eliminate paper is to do it at the source. I use a service called DocuSign in order to obtain legally binding documents that are digitally signed. This step eliminates the need to print documents, obtain signatures, and then scan them.

- Utilize PDF versions rather than printed documents where possible. My clients encourage the use of secure portals and PDF versions of data to streamline operations and enhance their client communication.

- Convert your fax line to a fax-to-e-mail service. You can reduce costs by eliminating a redundant phone line and printing only the documents that you absolutely have to print.

- Use existing staff to convert existing documents to digital by buying a good-quality scanner. If you do not have the resources to scan in-house, businesses exist that will help you scan documents at a very reasonable price.

- Capture and file receipts digitally with your smart phone's camera. Expensify is a great application for capturing data for you.

- Use www.shoeboxed.com. You (and your clients) can fill an envelope and send them directly to Shoeboxed. Shoeboxed will scan your data and store them in a secure online account, ready to be exported to your preferred accounting software.

2. Document Systems and Processes

Your ability to scale your business or grow is limited if you do not have effective documentation and training procedures in place for new staff.

- Tursa Group works with their clients to create short three- to five-minute videos on how to do almost every internal process in their company.

- The videos are shared with staff on a private YouTube channel.

- Staff access the videos by accessing links on an in-house intranet site.

- Complete documentation means that management is able to spend less time training employees.

- Training becomes on-demand and self-serve. Employees can find the information they need quickly without wasting time waiting for help.

- A variety of great software programs are available to capture video on your computer. Personally, I favor BB FlashBack (http://www.bbsoftware.co.uk). The Express version is free and has a lot of great features. Their paid versions are well worth the money if you are looking for additional features. The software captures the activity on your screen, and staff simply talk their way through their regular work. In this manner, your staff can document their daily duties without taking time away from productive work.

- The audio and video are saved in a video format and can be stored on a server, e-mailed, or uploaded to YouTube. For more confidential videos, I like the simplicity of Box.com for online collaboration and file storage.

3. Implement Cloud-Based Services

- Start planning now to implement cloud solutions over time. I do not recommend changing everything overnight; just make changes as you are able. If you have just spent money on server hardware, now is the time to plan so that you are ready for the cloud when your hardware is scheduled for replacement.

- Migrate your company to cloud-based solutions such as Google Apps, Office 365, Zoho CRM, Wave Accounting, Xero, etc. See appendix 4 for more examples of solutions that can help you as you grow your business.

- Cloud-based solutions allow you to eliminate your internal information technology infrastructure, significantly reducing information technology costs and improving reliability.

- With planning and forethought, you can implement hosted or custom solutions that will take your business completely into the cloud.

- Cost savings can be substantial, but the greater flexibility is probably the best feature of cloud-based solutions. You can work from any web-enabled device anywhere, anytime. One of my clients was able to access her client records from a beach in Cuba, solving a significant problem and allowing my client to return to her vacation.

- If you are reluctant to fully embrace cloud solutions, there is an intermediate step. You can use www.CloudLinx.ca as virtual computers. Your data are safe in the cloud, but you have your traditional programs installed on a computer that you can access from anywhere.

4. Outsource Tasks to Improve Efficiency and Flexibility

- *Outsourcing* is not a dirty word, nor is it the immoral act of taking jobs away from the North American economy. Using external computer support and having an external bookkeeper are common examples of local outsourcing. As a business owner, you owe it to your clients and your staff to build your business in a sustainable and efficient manner.

- Start by outsourcing mundane and repetitive commodity work. This practice frees up you and your staff to focus on value added services that require more client interaction.

- Segregate tasks that can be performed more efficiently by another person or organization.

- Outsourcing gives you the flexibility to scale up or down as demand for your services fluctuates.

- In-house staff can be freed up in order to do more meaningful tasks and enhance customer relationships by offering new services.

- You will see the most benefit from outsourcing if you integrate your outsourced staff into your company's culture and communication system. I have a virtual assistant in Mexico whom I communicate with on a daily basis, and she assists me with client interaction. The impact on freeing up my time has been amazing.

- Outsourcing fixes most of your file-related costs to an hourly rate—you know exactly how much you are paying and typically pay for only the time that you need.

5. Embrace Telecommuting as a Strategic Initiative

- If you embrace the previous steps, you can also implement telecommuting for your in-house staff. Telecommuting simply gives you the ability to work from anywhere. It is very similar to outsourcing, but staff still come in to the office as needed.

- Telecommuting will help you reduce office costs, and it can be used as a tool to recruit staff outside your local geographic area. This is especially important if you are in a small or remote community and need assistance with your workload. Local staff may simply be impossible to find.

- Telecommuting will work only if your organization has the right communication platform in place, such as a VoIP system and an internal chat system.

- Encourage members of your team to use the internal chat system to build relationships, whether they are physically in the office, are telecommuting, or are outsourced resources. This practice will provide a social outlet and give employees a place where they can seek help in order to complete tasks.

- Leverage online tools such as Box.com or Asana.com to facilitate integration and collaboration.

I have personally implemented all of these steps in my current business model, and I work with my clients to help them do so as well. My personal experience has been exceptional. There are many benefits, usually in relation to cost savings, but the most significant benefit for me is the freedom to work from anywhere at any time. I can now address issues as they arise and forget them, rather than wait to return to the office to resolve something.

Once you are paperless, you can realize even greater gains in your business by helping clients go paperless. Paperless clients means that you can share data easily and quickly. The back and forth to chase missing paperwork is eliminated. My motivation for going paperless was to completely eliminate the random boxes and bags of records that would sit in my office for months on end.

We will discuss consulting with your clients to take them paperless in more detail in Pillar 7, Value Added Services. You will find that the transition to a paperless office is actually a fairly simple process once you have been through it. You can integrate the paperless transition process into your bookkeeping practice as a new service to clients in order to build deeper relationships with your clients and charge higher fees.

Recap

In this section, we discussed how to improve operational efficiency in order to provide better service to clients and reduce operating costs. Digitizing your data, implementing project management, automating your work flow, and introducing alternative staffing arrangements are critical first steps. Increasing efficiency is a first step in making your bookkeeping business scalable and ready for exponential growth.

Project Management

Wikipedia defines the project management process as "the management process of planning and controlling in the performance or execution of a project." How is that definition relevant to a bookkeeping business? Once your data have been digitized, you can easily begin to manage your workload as a series of projects. Project Management Institute, Inc. (PMI), defines project management as "the application of knowledge, skills, tools and techniques to a broad range of activities in order to meet the requirements of a particular project."

Generally speaking, projects can be divided into five basic phases:

1. Project conception and initiation—identify projects that benefit the organization and determine whether or not a project is feasible and realistic.

2. Project definition and planning—this is usually the phase that is most likely to cause problems. If you do not properly define the project scope, you can end up with scope creep and unrealistic results. In this phase, project timelines and budgets are started.

3. Project launch or execution—official launch of the project, including distributing resources and determining team responsibilities.

4. Project performance and control—actual status for the project is monitored in comparison to expected timelines and budgets. Project managers are responsible for ensuring that resources are

properly allocated and monitored in order to keep the project on track.

5. Project close—once all tasks are completed and the client has approved the outcome, the team should evaluate the project to determine lessons that can be carried forward to subsequent projects.

Projects and project management processes vary by industry. These five basic phases are relevant in that they ensure that a project is properly conducted in order to solve a problem and provide future benefits to the organization. Too often, I see bookkeepers treating each client as a unique transaction. However, you can group certain aspects into common elements and manage the overall process as a project.

I personally use a project management approach for my internal projects and for my client work. Where possible, we break projects down into their component steps and work with our clients to ensure completion. Each project has an internal champion who is responsible for ensuring that tasks are completed on time and for pushing the projects forward.

I am currently using a virtual assistant whose sole responsibility is to manage projects. She updates me on the status of projects and keeps me up-to-date on areas that need my attention. We can identify bottlenecks and potential delays much faster because we have a deliberate focus on the big picture. We can avoid the client delays with a proactive approach.

We have adopted a fish bowl approach—our clients can see everything and know exactly what we are working on in their files. Perhaps more importantly, our clients know in advance if we will need something from them and they know if they are delaying the project. I don't normally like to point fingers or place blame, but a deliberate approach helps our clients keep things in perspective if they are the ones causing delays. Generally, this approach alone helps us avoid a lot of potential conflict.

There are a lot of great resources for project management. We use online project management courses to develop our team. I encourage internal training for more in-depth learning, so I have staff teach other team members about project management. The overall result is a stronger team with a greater breadth of knowledge.

The project management process can also be a valuable service that you can offer to your clients. For instance, if they are implementing a new software product, you can offer your project manager to facilitate the project and keep things on track. Not surprisingly, once our team had training in project management, we were able to identify opportunities and provide greater services to our clients.

We use two project management products. First, we use ProWorkflow to manage external projects. We chose ProWorkflow for its security and ability to grant secure access to our clients for their specific projects. ProWorkflow allows us to see all outstanding tasks internally and to share the client-specific tasks individually with our clients.

We use Zoho CRM to track our customer interactions and internal projects. Zoho CRM has a free version that requires you have a bit of knowledge to set it up properly. Their paid versions come with support and additional training. We use the free version because it was something we felt that we should learn ourselves. Zoho CRM allows us to track internal projects and tasks.

Asana receives honorable mention as a project management tool. They offer a free solution that can be integrated with your team and your clients. Asana has a paid version as well, which allows you to add a larger team.

Whether you implement the project management process internally, externally, or both, you will see great benefits in your business and for your clients.

Work Flow Automation

Work flow is simply how client work moves through your business. I am a strong advocate for documented internal systems and processes. Of course, systems and processes have to be monitored and enforced in order to ensure compliance and consistency.

The most common argument I hear from clients is that bookkeeping is client specific and cannot be standardized. I disagree but acknowledge that it comes down to how you define what you are standardizing.

Standardization should be applied to the process that guides work through your business at a high level. Work flow should have the same stages for all files, and everyone in the firm must follow the procedures. Be as specific as possible when creating and documenting systems and processes. The following are among the critical questions that your documentation must address:

- What is your marketing strategy?
- What is your sales cycle? Do you have guidelines for client acceptance?
- How do you initially receive work from the client? Who receives it? In what form do client records arrive?
- How is missing information handled? Who requests the additional information from the client? Who follows up? How often?
- What are your steps for handling and processing client records?
- What is your process for internal quality control on completed work?
- What is the client deliverable? Who prepares it? Who presents it to the client?
- Who bills clients for completed work? Is there a process in place to ensure that all completed work is properly billed?
- Do you have standard credit and collection policies? Are they followed?
- How is incomplete work tracked? Who follows up internally to determine timeliness of work completed within the firm? How often do you review the incomplete work?
- How are client and internal deadlines tracked and/or monitored?

The ultimate goal is to standardize internal systems and processes. Ideally, these should be formalized and documented in such a way as to allow staff to easily access the information.

I realize that each client and its needs may in fact be unique. However, every file ultimately goes through some process in which raw data are transformed into an end product. Consistency in the process will help you become more scalable and allow you to serve your clients better.

Standardization of the process will allow you to ensure consistency, accuracy, and completeness for all client work.

The time you invest at this stage will be repaid many times over if or when you hire new staff.

Tools

Documenting systems and processes can be a daunting task if you don't have the right tools on hand. We use the following tools to help our clients create documentation.

- ProWorkflow is our project management software. The first step is to create a project plan showing what needs to be documented and assigning accountability and responsibility to staff.

- XMind is software that allows you to easily create professional-looking organization charts, flowcharts, and mind maps.

- BB FlashBack Pro is used to record step-by-step tutorials and create a video record of how things should be done.

- Client Track is a full-featured practice management program. It has the ability to integrate your client database with a project management module, allowing quick and easy follow-up for missing information.

How?

Michael Gerber's book *The E-Myth for Accountants* is an excellent resource to start you on the path to standardization. For me, the starting point is to document how you currently do things. From here, identify areas of weakness or inefficiency. Work bottlenecks and supplementary spreadsheets are usually good indicators of problem areas.

Staffing Alternatives

If we look at most bookkeeping businesses, they fit into one of the following models for staffing:

- Traditional model—high overhead
- Telecommuting model—lower overhead
- Outsourcing model—still lower overhead
- Virtual model—nominal overhead
- Hybrid model—take the best of each

Traditional

The traditional employment model is more expensive than most business owners realize. Wages are just the beginning. Other costs include benefits, sick time, vacation time, office overhead, equipment costs (purchases and maintenance), and parking. If you don't have a good grasp of your costs, you may be leaking profit and not even be aware of it.

I realize that your overhead costs, especially rent, may seem fixed in the short term. I have worked with firms that have kept staff on just to minimize losses due to excess space. However, in many cases, you can rent out extra space or sublet the space and move into a smaller space. In other cases, firms struggle to do the work they have without hiring additional staff because they are out of space and do not have the time or inclination to consider a move.

Telecommuting and outsourcing are two options that can help you reduce overhead and still get work completed in a timely manner.

Telecommuting

If you use cloud solutions and eliminate paper, you are already on your way to telecommuting, at least from a technical perspective. The real challenge in telecommuting is to cultivate a corporate culture that builds strong staff relationships. Usually, management has to learn to trust that staff will continue to meet expectations and finish their work as required.

In my experience, staff appreciate the freedom to work remotely, so they will generally meet or exceed your expectations in order to continue telecommuting.

In one instance, I worked with a client that had a valued staff member with a unique double life. Her husband had moved to Vancouver for a very lucrative job, and she stayed behind in Calgary to continue with her job. I worked with the employer to implement telecommuting for this woman. In our initial arrangement, we set up a one-month trial period. The staff member would work remotely from Vancouver, and the employer would monitor her activities. It quickly became obvious that this particular staff member was far more productive being with her family. In the end, this became a permanent situation, and she comes to the office only for the occasional staff meeting.

One point of caution—implement telecommuting on a trial basis for any staff member who you think could do this. Not everyone can be productive in a home environment; it takes a unique type of person to ignore the distractions of home and focus on work. You will have a pretty good indication as to whether your trial is working if you watch staff productivity closely. For those staff who show more or the same productivity, encourage telecommuting. For those who don't maintain a reasonable level of productivity, bring them back into the office.

Personally, I implemented telecommuting as a means to free myself from the office and allow me to still work should something urgent require my attention.

I worked with one larger firm that leveraged telecommuting with dramatic improvements to their bottom line. They studied staff schedules for a period of time and realized that no more than 80 percent of their staff were consistently in the office at any point in time. This meant that roughly 20 percent of their desk space (and related overhead) was in essence spoiled inventory. The 20 percent absenteeism included a combination of time on-site with clients, sick leave, vacation time, and study leave.

The firm did minor renovations to their office and sublet roughly 15 percent of their space. In this case, they used external outsourcing and were very confident that they could continue to grow without adding more overhead or office space. Some of the remaining surplus space was repurposed to include meeting areas. Only partners and administrative staff had assigned desks. All others booked desk space using an internal reservation system. Meeting rooms became overflow space for staff on the rare occasion when the number of staff present exceeded desks available. Staff also had full authority to choose to work from home if they had deadlines to meet but didn't need to be in the office.

There were minor up-front costs, but ultimately the firm reduced their overhead by approximately 20 percent, and staff morale was vastly improved by their having a flexible work arrangement. An unexpected benefit was realized—the firm could now attract and retain remote staff outside their local geographic area.

Outsourcing

Outsourcing tends to have very negative connotations. Most of us probably use outsourcing or are the outsourcing agent without realizing it. Most small businesses use law firms to handle their legal affairs, external bookkeepers to manage their books, and external information technology consultants to manage their computer networks. These are all examples of business process outsourcing that we may even take for granted. If, however, you send that work outside North America, suddenly it is bad and taking jobs away from North Americans. The reality is that most of these jobs are already disappearing as we see more automation. It is becoming increasingly difficult to fill positions with staff who are willing to do mundane or repetitive work. Outsourcing is a viable solution because it gives jobs to people who want them.

I have actually seen outsourcing as a recruiting advantage for local firms. Students are more interested in a firm because they know they will be doing more interesting work and won't be stuck doing endless reconciliation projects. In my experience, firms that use outsourcing have higher morale—local staff are able to spend time on higher-level work and issues, thus keeping them engaged in their jobs.

I am not advising you to fire existing staff. If you have staff that you like and want to keep, you can offer them more interesting work. I see a lot of instances in which senior staff are able to develop and mentor junior staff better because they have the time to actually work with them. Juniors learn more because there are fewer junk files to complete.

Outsourcing has the following benefits and characteristics:

- can reduce costs and increase file quality
- is a scalable resource—adaptable to work volume
- locally based designated accountants focus on high-level issues
- time is spent identifying consulting opportunities, not on file preparation
- highest and best use of time—more focus on client meetings
- use in-depth conversations with clients to expand scope of work
- paperless office critical to success
- faster billing and collection

Payroll

Payroll is a subset of outsourcing, yet few consider it as such. The following are a few services that offer payroll outsourcing:

- Ceridian Canada—www.ceridian.ca
- Payment Evolution—www.paymentevolution.ca

- Payworks—www.payworks.ca
- Payweb—www.payweb.ca/costco/en/

This is not an exhaustive list. If you take the right approach, you can turn payroll into a profitable business development tool. Bring in a third party to administer payroll, and spend your time building relationships with your clients. Personally, I use Ceridian because they offer full-service payroll and human resources solutions as well.

Virtual

The virtual model takes eliminating overhead one step further by eliminating all physical staff and perhaps even the office. This is a great model if you are just starting out or if you are on your own and looking to slow down. We often forget how much work we actually have to do in order to cover our overhead.

The virtual model is a concept that requires you to be paperless and capable of telecommuting. The best way to start a virtual business is to rent a virtual office through one of the many business centers out there. I personally use Regus for my virtual office. The virtual office gives my clients a physical place to drop documents off, and I can book either meeting rooms or a day office for meetings. Depending on the service package, you generally have the ability to use the business center as a mailing address too. The business center covers all other overhead—they pay the receptionist, administrative staff, cleaning staff, Internet expenses, and even the costs of coffee! This is literally an instant business presence. The main advantage is that I pay for the facilities I need as I need them. I do not have any surprise costs or additional overhead.

The next step is to set up a virtual phone system. If you use Regus, they offer that as part of one of their packages. You can have incoming phone calls answered by the receptionist and redirected to wherever you happen to be. If your business center does not offer this service, you can look at a company like iTel. You can actually install a virtual phone on your computer and answer it just like a regular phone. The only requirement is that your computer have a microphone and speakers. If you don't have them, it is very easy to install a headset that will have both. Instant portable phone!

Paperless is one of the key concepts for working virtually. It makes things infinitely easier if you have full access to your records and client data. There are a few ways to go paperless. I took a shortcut and brought in Tursa Group to assist with the transition. I used them because they were already handling my information technology needs and I trusted them. If you prefer to do it by yourself, I recommend reading Roman Kepczk's book *Quantum of Paperless*. He provides a checklist for best practices and key considerations. Before you run out and buy scanners, I would recommend looking at local scanning services. It is often cheaper and faster to pay them to manage your digital data. Shoeboxed.com has a very interesting digitization service—you can have your clients send their records directly to Shoeboxed.com. You will receive a file that you can import into most accounting packages once the records have been digitized. This process saves a lot of time as you are reviewing and confirming transactions, saving the time normally spent entering them.

As you can see, it is very quick and easy to start a virtual presence. The main drawback is that not everyone can work remotely without the security of a dedicated office. In that case, the virtual model is not for you. If, however, you are able to work from anywhere, this model is perfect. The real advantage is that you don't get buried in an office away from your clients—you have more freedom to be portable, which often means you will visit client locations more often.

Hybrid

The hybrid model is not the same for everyone. It is, instead, a blend of the four other models in the combination that works best for your personal circumstances. For example, the traditional model is most appropriate if you have a full complement of staff and a long-term office space commitment. However, in that same scenario, you may look at telecommuting or outsourcing should your workload have high seasonal swings or if you have reached the physical capacity of your office space. Take a close look at your overhead, and think about creative ways to reduce it by applying the best of these models as they fit your needs.

Action Steps

- Commit to making a change in how you run your business.
- Read *Quantum of Paperless* by Roman Kepczyk as a guide to going paperless.
- Assess your business and its work flow to identify areas for improvement. Tackle the easy areas first to build momentum.

Pillar 2: Marketing and Networking

I have to admit that it has taken me considerable time to realize that sales and marketing are in fact two very different activities. Unfortunately, most businesses lump them together and miss opportunities as a result. Now that I understand the distinction, I will share my experiences in two separate Pillars.

As I see it, marketing involves activities that generate interest in your business, right up to the first contact between a prospect and your firm. I believe, then, that everything after the initial contact falls under the umbrella of sales. We will discuss sales in further detail in Pillar 3.

In my opinion, bookkeepers sell peace of mind. It is imperative that you realize how important it is to build trust and client relationships, as these are the foundation for keeping long-term clients. Your marketing efforts must set the stage for all future client interactions. First impressions will ultimately dictate future interactions with a new client.

Marketing can include any of the following activities:

- media and print advertising
- brochures
- signage
- website
- networking events
- educational events—seminars or webinars, including business-to-business interactions
- social media

In my experience, it is hard to stand out or make any significant gains through traditional marketing methods, such as television, radio, or newspaper advertisements. I believe the difficulties stem from the fact that mass media are exactly that—directed to the masses. For the most part, you target a medium's entire audience and hope that they identify with you.

Ideal Client

Before you do anything remotely related to marketing or networking, you have to know who your audience is. If you can create a clear picture of your ideal client, it is significantly easier for you to directly target your marketing efforts to them as a group.

I normally hear objections to this specialization from my bookkeeping clients. They argue that they can serve all industries and thus any client is a good client. I beg to differ—the specialist can always charge more than the generalist, so it makes sense to target a particular group. Technically, building a niche is part of marketing and thus could be discussed in detail here. However, because it covers many other aspects of your firm, a separate Pillar is directed specifically to niche development. For now, we will continue on the assumption that we all agree niche development or targeted marketing is important.

If you know your ideal client's characteristics, you are now in a position to market to them and reach out to them through networking events and channels.

Networking

Networking can be used for both marketing and sales. Ideally, it is an ongoing process repeated consistently to ensure a steady stream of new clients.

The unfortunate reality is that I often see a pattern emerge with bookkeepers. Initially, they are really successful because they have only a few clients and provide top-notch service. These clients, suitably impressed, reward the bookkeeper by referring friends, family, and colleagues. As the bookkeeping businesses grow, they either learn to manage the growing workload or they inevitably face a point where they are suddenly too busy. They are less responsive to clients and start to lose them just as quickly as they brought them in. Once the client base shrinks to a manageable level, the bookkeeper then exceeds service expectations and begins the growth phase again. The cycle repeats itself over and over, usually ending with the bookkeeper being frustrated, burnt out, and walking away from the business entirely.

If, on the other hand, you choose to make networking and growth part of your consistent plan, you can eliminate the ebbs and flows. Perhaps more importantly, you can use your marketing efforts to replace clients that you fire or you can use these efforts to build capacity for more staff. Either way, the more consistent you are, the more predictable your results.

In this Pillar, we will focus on networking specifically as a marketing tool. We will revisit networking in the sales Pillar to focus on its benefits in the relationship-building process for existing clients.

Before you consider networking, I highly recommend that you read about the process and prepare in advance. I often hear people complain that they didn't find any contacts at a particular event, so they gave up on networking. When I press further, I usually learn that the participant did not actually talk to anyone but instead stood in a corner waiting for prospects to come to him or her. Not a great strategy!

If you are serious about growth, I highly recommend that you take the time to read *Endless Referrals* by Bob Burg. Mr. Burg addresses a common problem with networking—too many people approach it from the perspective of "What's in it for me?" or "I need..." This attitude is off-putting in almost any situation; focus instead on the other person. Make a habit of asking others, "How can I help you?" Using this question alone has brought me many opportunities simply because my question disarmed the prospect and helped us move to a meaningful conversation instead of pointless small talk.

For the record, I do not consider myself a master of networking. I am good one-on-one, and I truly consider any event successful if I have a quality conversation with one good prospect. I prefer this method to attempting to make small talk with every single person present. This is merely my personal style; find the right blend that works for you.

Meetup.com is a great resource for finding local business events to attend. You register with their site and can then search interest groups to find ones that are appropriate for you. If you have done your homework and defined your ideal client, you can focus on a few groups. If you insist on being a generalist, you can literally spend the rest of your working life attending events chasing prospects.

I like to start groups, especially on Meetup, as it allows one to direct the conversation. Leading a group gives you instant credibility, and people will turn to you for solutions to common problems. Use this opportunity to grow by asking participants how you can help them grow.

A great growth strategy is to host business seminars in your boardroom. Invite a few key clients and ask them to bring along like-minded business associates. I normally offer these events for free, as I get a lot of referrals from them. You can either present a topic that you are knowledgeable about or bring in guest speakers. I see the most success with this approach if you are consistent. Make a point of creating a regular schedule, and use this as a way to form stronger relationships with existing clients and to expand your reach.

Follow-Up

We have discussed how networking can put you in the same room as your ideal clients and prospects. The next step is to actually do something with the information that you gather. Ideally, you should obtain business cards from everyone that you network with. A good habit is to write reminders on their cards as to what you discussed—helping them solve a problem is a great reason for following up after an event.

I will admit that when I first started networking, I made every possible mistake. The biggest one was taking people's business cards and not following up. I would have great intentions, piling the cards near my computer so that I could follow up. Paper would come and go across my desk, eventually either burying the business cards or pushing them into a "black hole," never to be seen again. Letting time pass before following up essentially meant I was cold-calling again.

My new habit is to get the contact details and the answer to "How can I help you?" into my Customer Relationship Management (CRM) software. Salesforce.com, SugarCRM, and Zoho CRM are all great programs with different features and price points. I personally use Zoho CRM because it has a great starter package, free for the first three users. Setup time is minimal, and it is easily accessible from any device.

Regardless of the CRM that you choose, it should be able to do the following:

- track leads and prospects
- monitor conversion rates
- maintain notes about the prospect
- track follow-up and action items for each prospect
- allow you to consistently quote fees to increase margins

I recommend a cloud-based CRM so that you can take notes in real time—I usually do this in the car before I leave an event. This practice keeps things fresh in your mind, and prospects really appreciate a prompt follow-up if you promise them information.

I know that most practice management programs recommend that you use their product to track your prospects. I am a purist; I believe that leads should be kept separate from your regular client lists for two simple reasons:

- Networking can generate a large volume of prospects, which can increase the size of your database—slowing performance.
- Commitments and follow-up for prospects can be delegated. The sheer volume of activity can overshadow your work tasks if you mix them in the same place.

Action Steps

- Create a marketing plan for your firm, including a budget as to where you will direct your efforts and how much you will spend.
- Identify your ideal client. Document this in detail.
- Select and implement a Customer Relationship Management solution to support your marketing efforts.

Pillar 3: Sales

As we discussed in Pillar 2, sales and marketing are distinct activities. If you prefer, reframe the word *sales* to encompass the role of relationship manager. Your sales process should flow naturally from your marketing efforts.

Do not expect instant results; marketing and networking are a lot like farming—you work hard, plant the seeds, and then have to wait until it is harvest time. Impatient people seldom see the value in the process if they can't see instant results.

Likewise, your sales efforts may not necessarily yield instant results. The real point to the sales process is to build deeper client relationships and to identify all of your clients' business needs. You can learn a lot about your clients by talking with them and then using the knowledge you gain to tailor value added services to them.

ProfitCents (https://www.profitcents.com) is one of my favorite sales tools. It is a cloud-based service that creates full-color reports indicating the client's relative financial health in comparison to industry data. I use ProfitCents as a discussion piece if I want to get to know a particular client better. I normally prepare the first report for free and use it as a great reason to meet with the client again. We review the report with the client, and inevitably there is an area that should be improved or the client will raise concerns. From there, you need a sales process to ensure that the client receives additional help. For the record, I do not expect that we are all experts in every aspect of business. Instead, I use my networking contacts to help my clients find the best solutions for them. Sadly, most bookkeepers will simply say that they don't know the answer and leave it to the client to solve the problem. Offering an alternative builds rapport with the client.

Once clients see that you are able to offer comprehensive information about their business, it is usually an easy conversation to encourage them to pay you to review their business on a quarterly basis. This becomes a value added service, and it also brings discipline and structure to your client relationship—at a minimum, they bring in their records quarterly, rather than at random intervals.

Create a deliberate sales process around the ProfitCents reports. They are the spark that ignites many an impassioned business conversation. Clients may forget what the report says in detail, but they will remember how impressed they were with your knowledge of their business.

The key to client relationships is taking the time to listen and to offer real solutions, not standard answers. Many tools exist that can assist you with this process.

I also find cash-flow conversations to be a good source of additional work. My process is fairly simple. I use their existing accounting software to generate monthly profit-and-loss figures for their most recent fiscal year. We export this report to Excel and offer it to the client as a low-cost budget. Technically, this is not a true budget and very little time goes into preparing it. There is a reason for this, as we want the client to appreciate our efforts. The next step is a quick overview as to how to prepare a detailed budget. Clients are given homework and asked to complete a budget on their own. After a couple of weeks of follow-up and client excuses, clients are generally ready to pay someone else to do it for them. At this stage, they are convinced that they need a budget and are willing to pay someone to prepare it for them.

PlanGuru (http://www.planguru.com) is my favorite tool for preparing budgets and cash-flow analysis. Excel has its place, but it is really best for simple businesses that have only one or two segments. Anything more complicated requires more flexibility than Excel provides. PlanGuru is a great tool built specifically for budgeting. They have a lot of assumptions built in and allow you to make fairly major changes to your model with a few simple selections. It is easy to review and update budget logic on the fly. PlanGuru really shows its strength if you have a business with multiple segments. You can actually prepare divisional or segment budgets and then consolidate them into a total entity budget. You can do a lot of "what-if" analysis by changing assumptions at the divisional level, which quickly flows through to the consolidated budget.

Normally, I see cash-flow discussions leading to additional projects, usually involving financing or systems and processes. Get comfortable with cash-flow conversations, as they will be your best sales tool. They will help you build client relationships and identify additional areas for improvement in the business.

Your sales function should be supported by your value added services (Pillar 7) and by your niche development activities (Pillar 4). We will discuss these concepts in further detail in subsequent Pillars.

Action Steps

- Identify value added services that you can offer to existing clients.
- Create a process to ensure that your services are offered consistently.
- Evaluate staff strengths to determine training or cross-training requirements for new services.

Pillar 4: Niche Development

Arguably, niche development could be included in the Pillars on marketing or sales, as it is really part of the growth through client acquisition strategy. However, niche development is relevant to all areas of growth, so I feel that it deserves a Pillar by itself.

I often confuse bookkeepers when I ask them to describe their ideal client. I know that this is an annoying question, and it is hard to see how it can be relevant to be selective if you are simply looking to grow. At some stage, we have collectively been misled into believing that all clients are good clients. False beliefs like this may be holding you back.

If you want to test this theory, look back at your earnings for the past year and compare your results to the information in the following table.

Key Performance Indicator	Rationale	Recommended Targets or Range
Percentage of new clients referred by current clients	Client referrals are a good measure of client satisfaction	10 percent or greater
Percentage of fees from new clients	New clients are relevant in determining growth potential	20 percent or greater
Percentage of fees from new services to existing clients	Measures organic growth by adding new services, which indicates the level of innovation within the firm	20 percent or greater

Total number of top clients required to generate 20 percent of your revenues	The smaller this number, the more concentration you have in your client base	Twenty or fewer for corporate clients
Total number of next tier of clients required to generate the next 20 percent of your revenues	The smaller this number, the more concentration you have in your client base	Fifty or fewer for corporate clients
Total number of remaining clients that generate the final 60 percent of your revenues	A high number can be indicative of inefficiencies in the firm	One hundred or fewer for corporate clients
Subjective assessment as to which of the three client groups (top 20 percent, next 20 percent, and bottom 60 percent) consume the most firm resources	Tying firm resources to firm revenues allows you to determine where your profitability can be found	Varies—most likely the bottom 60 percent will consume a disproportionate amount of firm resources.

What we tend to see time after time is that the top 40 percent subsidize the bottom 60 percent. I expect that you will find the same if you honestly review your numbers.

Pillar 8 goes into detail as to how to rank and fire clients. For now, take my word that the fastest way to grow is to make space in your business by eliminating your worst clients. Or, even better, don't take my word for it—experiment for yourself. Start small and fire your most disruptive and unprofitable client. Just fire one, and see how it impacts you and your firm. Sometimes one is all it takes to get the momentum started. If you are reluctant to fire a client, start even smaller by turning down a potential client that you think may become a problem client. In this case, you are literally out nothing, and it is far easier to stop problem clients at the door than to try to get them to leave later.

Before full panic sets in, evaluate how much future revenue you will lose and how much time you will recapture by firing one client. We will look to replace the lost revenue with more profitable work through niche development.

If you look at the bulk of human endeavors, the specialists often thrive while the generalists struggle. For example, tax specialists can charge significantly more for a basic tax return than a generalist can, merely because the client places a higher perceived value on the return prepared by the specialist.

The good news here is that it is very easy to become a specialist and start charging higher fees. The first step goes back to my annoying question, "What is your ideal client?"

Ideal Client

As we discussed in Pillar 2, your ideal client should always be the starting point for your future growth plans. After all, if you are going to grow, don't you want to grow with the right clients? Be as specific as possible when you define your ideal client. Focusing on a well-defined narrow segment of the population actually simplifies marketing, sales, and all other aspects of building a business. The key is to paint a clear mental picture defining all aspects of your ideal client. A fuzzy picture or lack of clarity will produce unreliable and unpredictable results. Your picture is incomplete until you can answer the following questions:

- What defines my ideal client? Is it industry, region, service line, etc.?
- What is the size of my ideal client?

- Are my ideal clients owner managed, professionally managed, or other?
- Are my ideal clients stand-alone businesses or franchises?
- Who are their largest vendors?
- Do they have a niche of their own?
- How are they trained?
- Where do they gather? Do they have an industry magazine, association, or annual conference?
- Do they require ongoing training for their business? If so, who offers that training?
- What is the biggest challenge in their niche?
- What specialized knowledge will you require to assist them? Do you have it, or can you obtain it?

This list is not exhaustive; it is just meant to demonstrate that you need to get very specific. Once you can answer these questions, you can start to look at marketing and sales.

Marketing to a niche is extremely easy. If you have determined their interests, training background, and ongoing affiliations, you can reach out to them directly. I will use dentists as an example on how to specifically build a niche. You can follow along step-by-step in appendix 5. As an aside, I usually recommend a niche that deals with professional service providers. They have been through extensive education and know what their time is worth; they will pay you well for your services if you can alleviate their business pain.

Action Steps

- Determine a niche for your business. If you already have a cluster of clients in the same industry, consider whether this is a niche that you want to develop deliberately.
- Review the current performance of your business.
- Clearly define your ideal client.

Pillar 5: Value Pricing

Value pricing is a very easy concept to understand, but it becomes a bit complicated to actually implement. The biggest obstacle to implementation is usually the self-limiting bias of the service provider.

Traditional accounting firms and bookkeeping businesses use some version of cost-plus pricing based on hours worked and a standard charge-out rate. There are several flaws to traditional pricing. In my opinion, the most significant flaws are as follows:

- You are penalized if you implement systems and technology to improve your efficiency. In theory, this means that you will work fewer hours to perform the same work as a less efficient firm. Yet billing per hour rewards the inefficient firm.

- There is an inherent conflict of interest between you and the client. The client focuses on how many hours you work and your rate, attempting to minimize both. You, on the other hand, are inclined to maximize both your hours and your rate.

- The focus for billing is on the cost to produce the product, not the value that the product produces for the client. Fees are often lower than what clients would be willing to pay if they considered the value.

Value-based pricing is very different. The client is charged a fee based on the value that they ascribe to the service. In a pure value-based pricing environment, each client's maximum value would be determined and fees would vary by client. Extensive economic theory lies behind the stages of value-based pricing, but we won't go into that in detail, as it has been extensively documented in several key books.

I like to simplify value pricing for my clients. Spend time with your clients in order to determine what their needs are. Identify the pain points in their business, and focus on solutions that will solve the pain. These are the solutions that the client is most willing to pay for. Based on your discussions, you can have clients identify what value they would place on a solution, and you use that as a starting point to fix your fee. That is right—you provide the client with a fixed-fee quote up front. By providing certainty around billing, you reduce risk for the client, and you can charge a premium. I encourage my clients to break a client's fee into monthly payments, which helps cash flow for both parties and eliminates collection risk. You can read a free e-book, written by Mike McDerment, called *Breaking the Time Barrier* for a great explanation of value pricing. McDerment uses a storytelling approach to explain the concept in plain English. The e-book is only seventy pages long, so it is a very high-level and quick introduction to implementing value pricing.

My intent has been to introduce the concept of value pricing and encourage you to do further research. Ronald J. Baker is, in my opinion, one of the leading advocates for value pricing. He founded the VeraSage Institute, and his stated mission is "to, once and for all, bury the billable hour and timesheet in the professions." He has written and co-written several books on the topic of value pricing and the overall management of professional service firms:

- *Professional's Guide to Value Pricing*

- *Implementing Value Pricing: A Radical Business Model for Professional Firms*

- *Pricing on Purpose: Creating and Capturing Value*

- *The Firm of the Future: A Guide for Accountants, Lawyers, and Other Professional Services*

- *Measure What Matters to Customers: Using Key Predictive Indicators (KPIs)*

I recommend reading all of these books to get a stronger grasp of the concepts. However, if you have limited time, the easiest and most productive use of your time would be to read *The Firm of the Future*. Mr. Baker covers the topic very well and reduces the discussion to easily understood language. *Implementing Value Pricing* has become the de facto textbook for professional services firms that are serious about implementing value pricing. It is a great book and is highly informative. However, it contains a fair bit of economic theory and it takes some effort to work your way through it. Again, it is time well spent, but it still takes time.

In my experience, using value pricing is one of the fastest ways to strengthen your client relationships and increase the fees that you charge. Assuming that you have completed your homework for the previous Pillar, you now have a clear picture of your ideal client. Value pricing is now significantly easier to implement because you will be producing more focused and predictable work as a specialist. If you have properly positioned yourself as an industry expert, you can now charge higher fees for traditional services and introduce value added services at a premium.

Action Steps

- Download and read *Breaking the Time Barrier* from http://breakingthetimebarrier.freshbooks.com.
- Create an action plan to implement value pricing.

Pillar 6: Technology

Technology could be considered part of operational efficiency. I would agree if we were just discussing the standard technology and commonly used solutions. I am separating technology into a Pillar on its own so that we can focus on disruptive technology that will change how we work. I am deliberately omitting discussion about technology designed to maintain the status quo by streamlining inherently flawed processes.

In this Pillar, we will look at the following areas and how they can be disruptive and advance your business:

- cloud solutions
    - what is the cloud?
    - cloud vendors
    - cloud security
    - core benefits of cloud computing
    - examples of cloud-based Software as a Service
    - examples of cloud-based communication tools
- virtual server
- personal workstations

Cloud Solutions

- Cloud computing is essentially a metaphor for the Internet. For our purposes, we will discuss three versions of cloud solutions.

- "Pure" cloud solution—no installation is required; you run the program completely within your web browser. Your browser navigation allows you to work your way through the program.

- "Hybrid" cloud solution—some installation is required in order to run your program. Generally, this is just an interface to facilitate access. For example, if you use Citrix's GoToWebinar, a small installation is required to access the actual webinar. The bulk of the processing is done on the cloud side.

- Virtual desktop installation—standard desktop applications are installed on a virtual PC located on a cloud-based server. For example, CloudLinx (https://www.cloudlinx.ca) provides a solution in which you can install QuickBooks or Sage 50 directly on a virtual PC. You can then log in and access the programs literally from any Internet-enabled device—smart phone, tablet, PC, Mac, and even Linux machines.

What Is the Cloud?

According to Wikipedia, "The Cloud, or Cloud Computing, is a term used to refer to a model of network computing where a program or application runs on a connected server or servers rather than on a local computing device."

In plain English, that essentially means that the end user connects to a remote server (or servers) in order to perform tasks. I see this as technology coming full circle, returning to the days of the mainframe and dummy terminal. However, the access and processing speeds are far superior.

The term *cloud* came into common use to describe the cloud computing infrastructure due to the common practice of using a cloud symbol to denote unknown segments of a network in network diagrams. Essentially, the cloud originally included all components external to the physical location of the business.

You can have one of the following deployment models for your cloud solution:

- private cloud—dedicated resources for your needs, behind a corporate firewall
- public cloud—shared resources available to the public over the Internet
- community cloud—resources shared between organizations
- hybrid cloud—combination of private, public, and/or community resources

Within each of these deployment models, there are several variations in terms of service models:

- Software as a Service (SaaS)—software is licensed on a subscription basis and is centrally hosted on the cloud
- Infrastructure as a Service (IaaS)—physical or virtual machines are shared via the cloud
- Platform as a Service (PaaS)—the consumer creates an application or service using tools from the provider

All "as-a-service" offerings have low initial cost, incremental cost based on usage, self-service, and a great degree of scalability.

Cloud Vendors

The following companies represent key players in the current cloud environment. Their offerings include a variety of these deployment and service models:

- Amazon
- Citrix
- Google
- IBM
- Microsoft
- Oracle Cloud
- Rackspace
- Zoho

Cloud Security

Theoretically, the centralization of data allows greater concentration of security resources. Conversely, this also means that hackers may have greater success because they can focus on one security platform as opposed to several. The reality is that most data breaches are the result of internal issues and disgruntled employees, not random hackers on the Internet.

With the cloud, there are a few issues and advantages:

- Less control over data—your contractual relationship with your cloud provider will determine who has access to your data and under what circumstances.

- Regular software updates to fix bugs—regular updates enhance your data's security, reducing the risk that unfixed bugs will cause security weaknesses. In addition, all users have the same version because updates are completed automatically.

- Physical security—I guarantee that any major data center is more secure than a server in your office. I say this with certainty because I often see servers in odd places, including broom closets and lunchrooms. I have seen very few offices that have their server in an environmentally controlled room with enforced access restrictions. The greatest risk to servers in most practices that I see is the risk of physical damage due to water leakage or extreme heat. In a data center, they deliberately build the space to accommodate computer equipment. The buildings are climate controlled, with antistatic measures and restricted access to the equipment. Most large centers are located in anonymous buildings—they do not advertise where they are located. Last, the data centers generally have a swarm of technicians hovering over the equipment to ensure maximum uptime.

- Encrypted data—regardless of where you store your data, it should be encrypted. I would argue that this is as important on a laptop or desktop as it is in the cloud because local computers can easily be stolen. I once worked in an international accounting firm. A person walked into the building with a utility cart and proceeded to pick up unattended laptops from staff desks. None of the staff noticed the thief until computers were discovered to be missing. Replaying security footage showed several staff members walking past the thief in action. No one challenged him or even paid any attention to what he was doing. Replacing the laptops was annoying, but the real loss was the client data that were not encrypted and therefore subject to unauthorized access. Breach of data is a serious threat to the survival of a firm; clients will not trust you if you expose their confidential information. In the cloud, you want to make sure your data are encrypted as they move to and from your cloud solutions, and even while stored in the cloud.

If you deal with a cloud service provider, you should ask the following questions:

- Who has access to your data?
- Are your data encrypted? Who has the encryption keys?
- Who owns your data? If you leave your cloud solution, can you take your data with you?
- What certifications or compliance standards are they following? Ensure that the levels are appropriate for your individual needs.

Core Benefits of Cloud Computing

- nimble
- efficient
- readily available
- cost-effective
- flexible
- scalable
- gives users access to enterprise-level applications
- secure
- eliminates expensive physical servers
- automatic updates—hardware and software

- quick and easy collaboration between clients and staff
- instant access to information
- access information anytime, anywhere
- reduce overhead—hardware, software, energy, and office space
- business continuity
- consolidated data
- technical support handled by provider
- integration of document scanning—consulting opportunities
- timely information

Examples of Cloud-Based Software as a Service

- Zoho Books (https://www.zoho.com/books)—accounting package
- ShareFile (http://www.sharefile.com)—alternative to a client portal; allows you to share data securely over the Internet
- Xero (www.xero.com)—accounting package
- Wave (www.waveapps.com)—accounting package
- FreshBooks (www.freshbooks.com)—accounting package
- Kashoo (www.kashoo.com)—accounting package
- Expensify (www.expensify.com)—expense reporting tool
- ProWorkflow (www.proworkflow.com)—project management and tracking software

I am often asked which online accounting package is the best. I hate to be vague, but the best answer truly depends on your needs. Each of the above programs has been designed with specific end users in mind. If you pair the right software with your client base, you will see great results. If you ignore the intentions of the developer, you will get random results at best.

Examples of Cloud-Based Communication Tools

- GoToMyPC (http://www.gotomypc.ca)—remotely access your computer through the Internet
- GoToMeeting (www.gotomeeting.ca)—organize and host virtual meetings online
- GoToWebinar (http://www.gotomeeting.ca/webinar)—a larger-scale option, allowing more participants
- GoToTraining (http://www.gototraining.com)—large-scale platform to facilitate online training
- Join.me (join.me)—virtual meeting tool, allowing for screen and file sharing
- AnyMeeting (www.anymeeting.com)—virtual meeting tool for screen and file sharing
- Google Hangouts (plus.google.com/hangouts)—virtual meeting tool for screen and file sharing; you can upload your recorded sessions directly to YouTube to allow for ongoing sharing
- YouTube (www.youtube.com)—you can create public or private videos to allow for training and collaboration
- Skype (www.skype.com)—virtual meeting tool for screen and file sharing
- Prezi (prezi.com)—cloud presentation tool; generally considered an alternative to Microsoft PowerPoint
- DocuSign (www.docusign.com)—tool to manage digital signatures

Virtual Server

I personally take a radical approach. I believe that the traditional on-site server is an anchor to your office. A physical server can impede staff mobility and prevent staff from bonding with clients by working on-site.

I agree that there are great solutions that will allow you to remotely access your server in the office. However, there are several points for potential failure:

- Internet connection
- routers and switches
- server access—potentially disrupted by either hardware failures or software problems

Cloud solutions won't take these issues away, but they do minimize their impact. In a worst-case scenario, you can access the Internet from a local coffee shop, giving you full access to your data. With a hardware failure in the traditional server scenario, someone usually has to be physically present to fix the problem and there is the added potential for downtime if you have to wait for replacement parts.

If you are not ready to go completely into the cloud for all of your technology needs, you may want to consider a virtual cloud server to reduce ties to your office. The virtual server functions much like your traditional physical server. However, it is actually based in an external data center, monitored and maintained around the clock by dedicated information technology professionals. Hardware failures are generally irrelevant, as these centers have the ability to switch you over to new hardware, often without any downtime. The maintenance people also focus on preemptive maintenance, not reactionary maintenance. This approach further protects the integrity of your data. The data centers have redundant Internet connections, so you will rarely experience downtime.

Advantages of a virtual server over a physical server include the following:

- Fast setup for new employees—local machines are basically dummy terminals; no installation is required before the computer is given to a new employee.
- Scalable—à la carte computing allows you to pick and choose the components that you need, making it possible to determine the balance between performance and cost that best suits your needs.
- Nominal up-front investment for virtual server—you pay monthly as you go. This arrangement is generally better than the large up-front investment required to purchase and install a physical server.
- Disposable staff computers—no software is installed, and no data are stored on the computer. You can easily replace a computer within minutes should it be lost, damaged, or stolen.
- Greater security—no data are stored on local computers or shared via flash drives.
- I used SysGen (www.sysgen.ca) and RackForce (rackforce.com) to set up my virtual server

If you have a server that is working well, by all means keep it in service. However, if it is approaching the end of its life cycle, now would be a great time to investigate whether a virtual server would be more beneficial. Unfortunately, there is an inherent conflict of interest between most information technology providers and their clients. They make their money by selling and maintaining physical equipment. Selling you a physical server provides them with a predictable revenue stream over the server's life. On the other hand, leveraging a virtual server to help your organization brings them a small setup fee, but it deprives them of their margins on the hardware sales and reduces their monthly maintenance revenues too.

I am not accusing the industry of improper business practices, just indicating that there is a significant downside to them if they recommend a virtual solution as opposed to a physical solution. The other drawback with the industry is that they tend to create a standard server model package and sell it over and over again. They become very adept at installation and maintenance, but they fall behind in the area of innovation. Innovation, in fact, decreases their productivity and profitability. By design, information technology professionals sell older solutions for the simple reason that they are the easiest to maintain, regardless of what is actually in your best interests.

Personal Workstations

I will make one concession and talk briefly about traditional personal computers, as I am often asked what people should be looking for when they purchase individual workstations. If you have a virtual server or are cloud-based, the question becomes irrelevant, as you need minimal computing power to reach your cloud resources.

If you are not yet in the cloud, you should consider the following:

- Windows 7 versus Windows 8.1—there is a definite learning curve to Windows 8.1. If you have a computer with Windows 7, I would recommend staying with it at least until you are comfortable with Windows 8.1. To get that level of comfort, consider upgrading a home computer before you upgrade your workstation. I personally prefer most of the features in Windows

8.1. There are still a few bugs, but they should be worked out in the coming months.

- I suggest at least a minimum of 4 gigabytes (GB) of Random Access Memory (RAM). This will allow you to run most programs currently on the market. If, like me, you are impatient, I would suggest 6 GB or more. My current computer has 16 GB, but that is overkill for the average user.

- I suggest i3 or i5 processors, but go for an i7 if you are willing to pay more for better performance.

- 32-bit versus 64-bit—this is really relevant only if you have more than 4 GB of RAM. If you have more than 4 GB, you will need a 64-bit processor in order to get the most utility out of your RAM. If you have 4 GB or less, you will be fine with a 32-bit processor.

- Laptop versus desktop—whether you think a laptop or a desktop is the best computer, you are right. For this decision, you need to consider how you will personally work. If you are office bound and never venture outside of the office to work, then you would probably prefer a desktop. You can get additional power at a lower cost if you look at desktops. Desktop models also allow you to easily add multiple monitors. If, on the other hand, you are highly portable and spend most of your time working outside the office, then a laptop is likely better for you.

- How many monitors—I generally recommend somewhere between two and four monitors, depending on the type of work that you do. If you are merely doing data entry, two monitors will be sufficient. If you are doing more complicated tasks, such as preparing tax returns and financial statements, you will see more productivity with four monitors. The key here is to ensure that your staff have some guidance on how to best utilize and place their additional monitors. Bad habits can be created if staff do not have some guidance.

- Data backup versus archival—a lot of firms that I encounter struggle with data backup because their data are intermingled. We typically keep our data long after we should, thus building up the size of our data files. Your data can be at rest or active. At rest data are the historical data that should never change—including files for previous years, permanent files, etc. Active data are the data that will change, including files for the current year. If you separate the two, you can create one archive for the historical at rest data. This setup significantly improves your backup and restore routine's speed because there are fewer files to process. If you can streamline backup, there are many great cloud solutions that will ensure you never lose a file again.

I can't stress enough how important it is to consider how you and your team will be working when you make information technology decisions. The needs of a portable road warrior are far different from those of a desk-bound staff member.

Action Steps

- Review your information technology plan for the next year. Determine which, if any, of the listed cloud solutions could enhance your business.

- Encourage conversations about cloud solutions with your clients. Ask them for their thoughts and recommendations in regards to technology.

Pillar 7: Value Added Services

Eliminating inefficiencies and automating work flow should show you the potential in your business. You will see the most significant growth once you look at the services that you offer to your *ideal clients* and introduce the services that they need the most.

Focus groups and extensive market research may be useful tools for determining client needs, if you have time on your hands and money to invest in the process. Short term, you can get a reasonably accurate assessment by simply asking your current *ideal clients* what they find most stressful in their daily business affairs. The symptoms usually form a pattern, which will ultimately lead you to a short list of the services that they need most.

At this point, I will emphasize that your growth is centered on *ideal clients*. Continue to maintain your existing clients, but focus your growth efforts on *ideal clients* only.

Your goal is to identify high-pain areas that you can help resolve. The greater your clients' pain, the more they will be willing to pay for your services—they will place a higher perceived value on someone who solves their biggest challenges. As an analogy, migraine sufferers will pay more to ease their pain than someone with a hangnail. You are becoming an expert in your niche; offer expert solutions that will directly benefit your niche. Get creative in finding ways to solve pain specific to your niche. Here are a few potential services that you can offer. Tailor the specific solutions to your niche.

I suggest the following value added services to consider. Your choice, of course, will be dictated by your personal skill set and willingness to learn.

- Cash flow—as we discussed in Pillar 3, PlanGuru (www.planguru.com) is a great tool for building meaningful cash-flow budgets. This becomes a starting point for recommending many other services.

- Financing packages—ProfitCents (www.profitcents.com) and PlanGuru can be used to help your clients create financing packages for their banks. Word of caution—specific rules apply to the preparation of information for banks. Offer this service only if you are familiar with the requirements specific to your background.

- Quarterly updates—ProfitCents generates a great report that shows strengths and weaknesses in your clients' financial numbers. Review these quarterly with your clients. Again, these meetings are an excellent way to charge additional fees and identify more services that you can offer.

- Business mentoring—by default, the average bookkeeper sees a lot more businesses in action than the typical business owner, who may only ever see their own business in operation. A lot of resources are available that allow you to provide business mentoring to your clients. At the very least, I recommend webinars to train clients in areas such as business basics, record keeping, and deductibility of expenses.

- Wealth management—more firms are starting to enter the realm of wealth management. This is a highly specialized area and should be entered with the assistance of properly qualified people. At the very minimum, you can confirm that the current wealth manager is in fact reporting accurate results to your clients. You become a second set of eyes reviewing results to protect your clients' interests.

- Succession and transition planning—if there is a business, odds are excellent that some sort of transition will happen. Businesses can be passed to the next generation, sold to key personnel, sold to external parties, or shut down. Oddly, most clients do not even realize that these are their only four options. If you are comfortable, recommend planning and preparation for an eventual transition. If you are not, bring in a local expert to talk to your clients about transition. Either way, clients will appreciate that you actually had the conversation with them.

- Business brokerage—the rules surrounding business brokerage are complex and vary by jurisdiction. I recommend that you do a bit of due diligence so that you can at least provide your clients with basic information. You can either become a business broker yourself or build relationships with local brokers. In many cases, they will actually pay you a referral fee if you bring them a client.

- Data management—clients going through a transition have unique needs for data management, as they have to provide support for due diligence in the transaction. You can work with your clients to provide and organize the information. This can be a lucrative engagement if you have multiple suitors for a business.

- Project management—bookkeepers tend to be more organized than most of their clients. You can use this gift to provide project management services for your clients.

- Payment handling—process accounts payable and monitor payments on behalf of your clients.

- Invoicing and collections—help your clients with their revenue cycle, offering invoicing solutions and assisting with collections.

- Management reporting—prepare special reports to support management decisions.

- Accounting information systems—create a true accounting information system that will assist your clients in gathering the information necessary to make key decisions.

- Management information systems—one step beyond accounting information systems, management information systems help your clients gather the information they need to properly manage their businesses.

- Paperless consulting—once you learn how to eliminate paper from your business, you are easily in a position to assist your clients with the same process. Create checklists and offer project management services to help clients reduce or eliminate paper.

Ultimately, this situation benefits you, as you have more options if your clients are paperless too.

- Software selection and implementation—with the onslaught of cloud solutions, the options are becoming far more complex and clients are struggling to make proper business decisions. You can assist by working with clients to determine their needs and help them with the transition.

- Controller—combining the above services in one form or another allows you to act as the external controller for your clients. Offering a higher level of service allows you to build deeper relationships and charge higher fees. Most bookkeepers fill the role of external controller. Right or wrong, clients perceive a higher value in the label *controller* than they do with the term *bookkeeper*. Train yourself and your staff to consistently use the title of controller. This shift will increase your perceived value and differentiate you in a crowded marketplace.

Action Steps

- Identify unique skills available immediately within your firm. Create value added services to best utilize these skills.

- Locate local professionals who offer complementary services and ask them to work on mutually beneficial projects.

Pillar 8: Practice Management

Practice management is a fairly broad term, so we will create a working definition for the purposes of this section. In my opinion, practice management is really just the conscious decision to manage the important variables in your bookkeeping business in order to maximize profit, manage your work flow, enhance worker satisfaction, and, perhaps most importantly, create a better client experience. In short, to do more work in less time while maintaining good working relationships with staff and clients.

That is a lot to ask, so we will break this approach down further into the following:

- critical success factors
- key performance indicators
- client selection and ranking

Critical Success Factors

Critical Success Factors (CSFs) are the essential tasks that your business needs to do well on a consistent basis in order to succeed. Based on this definition, you will see that you need to have a clear vision as to what it means for your business to succeed. The more specific you can be, the more accurately you can determine your CSFs. Success can mean any number of things to different people, so clearly define what it means for you, your business, and your team. An unclear target will yield imprecise results. As a business owner, you should ask yourself and your team what leads clients to choose your business in the first place and to stay with you. The answers to this question are usually the CSFs for a business. Review your own business to determine your CSFs. In my experience, the best CSFs for bookkeeping businesses revolve around the following:

- Customer satisfaction—we don't sell time or bookkeeping; we sell peace of mind. Therefore, our ability to instill confidence and reassure stressed-out clients will be very important. Perception becomes reality, so we need to ensure that our clients trust us.

- Pricing—you can compete to be the lowest-priced service provider in the market, be a midrange service, or focus on premium pricing. The pricing strategy you choose will impact your CSFs dramatically. A low-price provider focuses on speed and cost. A premium provider might focus on file quality.

- Accuracy—this is very important, but it is not the most important factor. Why? Clients care more about a relationship and how we fix errors, rather than about our avoiding them in the first place. I absolutely believe that you need excellent quality control. However, treating the client with respect and fixing errors promptly will often go further in a client's mind than not making mistakes at all.

- Staffing—if you have staff, clients are particularly sensitive to the number of people they interact with, especially if you are building your brand around a premium pricing model. You should strive to ensure that your most valuable clients have a consistent team to serve their needs.

There is an exchange in Alice's Adventures in Wonderland between Alice and the Cheshire Cat that I believe is the perfect metaphor for how most businesses approach planning:

> "Would you tell me, please, which way I ought to go from here?"
> "That depends a good deal on where you want to get to," said the Cat.
> "I don't much care where—" said Alice.
> "Then it doesn't matter which way you go," said the Cat.
> "—so long as I get somewhere," Alice added as an explanation.
> "Oh, you're sure to do that," said the Cat, "if you only walk long enough."

As you can see, if you don't know what your end goal is, everything is just a matter of being busy. This is not an effective way to run a business.

Once you determine your CSFs for your business, you need to use your current situation to create a road map to plot the shortest course to success from your current location. I like to use "SMART" goals with my team members and my clients. Different people use different words to define *SMART*, but I believe that the following will suffice for our purposes:

- Specific—what specific area will be improved?
- Measurable—is there a quantifiable measure of progress?
- Actionable—what action can be taken?
- Realistic—is the goal realistic with current resources and information?
- Time-related—when do you anticipate achieving the results?

SMART goals for your bookkeeping business might include the following:

- decrease average file turnaround time by 20 percent within the next six months by implementing systems and processes.
- increase average fee per file by 10 percent within the next year by adding new services to our product mix.
- reduce overhead by 12 percent in the next fiscal year by implementing alternate staffing solutions, such as telecommuting or outsourcing.
- decrease average file error rates by 15 percent in the next six months by improving the internal training program and sending the data entry team to external training courses.

Whether you are looking to increase something good or decrease something bad, you need to be SMART about goal setting if you want your goal to be more than just a wish. Once you have defined success for your business, you need to implement ways to measure your progress.

Key Performance Indicators

If Critical Success Factors are driving your strategy forward, you need to have a tool in place to measure your progress. That tool is found in Key Performance Indicators (KPIs). KPIs can answer questions such as the following:

- How close is the business to success at any given moment?
- Are we making progress toward our goals?
- Are we there yet?
- Should we give our staff bonuses this year?

Due to their nature, KPIs will be very different for different businesses. In fact, two bookkeeping businesses that appear identical on the surface may have different KPIs, leading to different results in the long term. Divisions or departments within the same bookkeeping business also will very likely have distinct KPIs. For example, marketing efforts are measured differently than quality control or data input.

At the risk of being repetitive, KPIs are crucial to determining how well your business is meeting the targets set for it in order to advance your Critical Success Factors. The specificity and accuracy of your critical success factors will impact what you need to measure, how you measure it, and what impact your management will have on outcomes.

Whenever I talk about KPIs, I take the liberty of going on a tangent to clarify the difference between efficiency and effectiveness. Efficiency is doing a particular task in the best way possible in order to achieve a result. Effectiveness is doing the right tasks in order to achieve a higher outcome. A business can be efficient, but if it is not effective, it is ultimately doomed to failure. An effective but inefficient business is far easier to salvage than an ineffective but efficient business. KPI selection is critical to ensure that you are focusing on effectiveness first and then on efficiency.

One word of caution about KPIs—I have worked with many business owners, and they all make the same mistake initially. They realize that they have been achieving random results by not measuring performance, so they go overboard and implement a broad range of KPIs. When it comes to fine wine and KPIs, less is truly more. Too many KPIs can cause unintended conflicts and overwhelm staff. You will see far better results if you initially prioritize and start with a few that will have the greatest impact on your business.

Key Stages to Creating KPIs

KPIs are essential for any business. When you are ready to create them:

- define your business processes
- set requirements for each business process
- use quantitative and qualitative measurements to compare current results with goals
- investigate variances and refine processes (or redistribute resources) in order to achieve goals

Typical KPIs for a professional services firm include the following:

- average fee per client
- file turnaround time
- lockup rate—days that work is tied up in either work in progress or accounts receivable
- gross margin
- profit margin
- billable hours
- realization rate—percentage of standard hourly rate collected
- staff satisfaction
- customer satisfaction

You will note that some of the KPIs listed are, in fact, hard to directly measure. Customer satisfaction is an example of a KPI that often has to be measured indirectly, sometimes by looking at attrition rates and client turnover. I have to admit that I have yet to go into an accounting firm that didn't have a multitude of KPIs to monitor and track. As I mentioned earlier, using too many KPIs can be detrimental.

Take the time to customize KPIs to your business, and you will see dramatic improvements; your time will not be wasted. Having a clear picture of your Critical Success Factors and KPIs will give you the confidence to be selective with your clients.

Client Selection and Ranking

Have you ever fired a client? If you have, you know that it was an intimidating experience, but I bet you also felt a huge sense of relief and satisfaction afterward. Truth be told, I have always enjoyed firing a client that didn't fit with my view of the firm. I felt it was my reward at the end of a long tax season, and I made it an annual event to fire the bad clients immediately after the deadline passed. It became a bonding experience for staff, as I allowed staff to nominate clients to be fired as well.

This concept may seem counterintuitive, but there is a point in your firm's growth where you cannot grow further unless you eliminate some of your clients. The Pareto Principle (also known as the 80/20 rule) applies in many cases. The short version is that 80 percent of your results come from 20 percent of your efforts. Similarly, 80 percent of your problems likely arise from 20 percent of your clients. The actual ratio might be 70/30 or 90/10, but over time, it usually gravitates to 80/20.

I encourage my clients to review their billings to determine who their top clients are and how much these clients contribute to the bottom line.

In most cases, we find that less than 20 percent of the clients contribute 80 percent of the business' profits. My clients usually object at this stage, as they refuse to believe that 80 percent of their effort is essentially wasted. However, I simply have to point out that we are reviewing the internal records they have prepared. I am not in a position to influence the results based on historical data.

For the record, I am not suggesting that you eliminate 80 percent of your client base in one fell swoop. I am, however, telling you that you will need to eliminate some clients in order to make room for bigger and better clients.

Before you can rank your clients, you need to have a clear picture as to what your ideal client looks like. Spend time reviewing the clients that you enjoy working with, the type of work you enjoy doing, and whom you want to spend your time with. Your ideal client should offer you the opportunity to do meaningful, interesting, and profitable work. Your ideal client characteristics will determine how you rank your clients and prospects. There are many ways to rank clients, and you can make this process as complicated as you like. For my practice, and for the businesses that I work with, we implement a very simple four-stage ranking:

- "A" clients—ideal clients that you enjoy working with; they possess all of the characteristics that you value in a client.

- "B" clients—these have most of your preferred characteristics but not all. They are still good clients, but they may need some coaching in order to become "A" clients.

- "C" clients have deficiencies, and they do not have the majority of your preferred characteristics. Again, they have the potential to become "A" clients, but only if you work to educate them.

- "D" clients are missing the vast majority of your preferred characteristics. They are easy to identify, as they are usually the ones that every person in your business complains about. You know the type—they bring doom and gloom to your team just by entering the office. The reality is that "D" clients are very likely complaining about you to prospects, and this causes more damage than firing them would.

When I work with businesses, regardless of the business type, the first step is to have them fire one "D" client. I am not doing it to be difficult; I just know that the first fired client is the hardest. Once my clients understand this idea, they often become very eager to start firing more clients.

At this stage, I usually advise my clients to take a more moderate course. I work with them to identify a few prospects that meet their "A" client criteria and pursue them. Once my clients bring in new work, we then commit to firing more "D" clients. As was mentioned above, this is not a one-to-one replacement; we can usually fire eight "D" clients for every new desirable client.

I have one client that was an extreme example. Overall, they had approximately two hundred clients, and their average fee size was about $1,000 (annual sales of approximately $200,000). When we reviewed their records, we were all surprised to discover that their top twenty clients generated sales of over $150,000. The remaining 180 clients were simply draining energy and wasting resources. This particular client fired all but their top twenty clients. This decision initially led to a dip in sales, but it didn't take long to replace the lost revenue by working to provide more and better services to their smaller client base. As you can see, the average fee per client is much higher if you eliminate the lower-end clients, increasing to $7,500 per client in the new reality.

In all fairness to my client, the larger clients grew gradually over time and just eclipsed the firm. It had become routine to service their clients as a collective, and fee concentration never came up as a topic of discussion. My client did not know that they could actually choose whom they worked with; they thought that it was their obligation to work with all clients and treat them equally.

I will offer two examples of an ideal client, and the resulting ranking scheme will vary based on client characteristics.

For our first example, I worked with a bookkeeper who had only one characteristic for her ideal client—payment of her fees. This becomes a very simple ranking. I will oversimplify to make a point. Her ranking was as follows:

- "A" clients paid their fees at the time service was completed—they brought payment to their meeting.

- "B" clients usually took up to thirty days to pay their account balance.

- "C" clients were generally prompt but occasionally took thirty to sixty days to pay their account.

- "D" clients took an extended period to pay and occasionally paid with checks that ended up being returned with insufficient funds. A collection agency or extreme leverage was needed to collect balances.

I will use my firm as the next example. I will stress here that I focused on business advisory services and avoided personal tax returns unless they had some connection to a corporate file. My ideal clients required business advisory services and minimal compliance work. Also, I work very closely with my clients, so personality fit and willingness to adopt change featured highly in my list of ideal client characteristics. I ranked my clients based on the following:

- "A" clients were fun to work with, provided me with interesting challenges, and required a variety of business advisory services.

- "B" clients were still fun to work with and provided interesting challenges, but they didn't need a broad range of business advisory services.

- "C" clients did not require any business advisory services, only corporate compliance work.

- "D" clients were clients that I did not enjoy working with or just required personal income tax work.

As you can see, your biases and preferences will impact which clients you should work with. In my case, I made the conscious decision to fire my "C" and "D" clients. I wanted to focus on business advisory services, so I eliminated the bulk of my clients. I offered a broad range of premium services, which meant that I didn't notice much of an impact on my business. We quickly recovered from lost revenues by focusing on a few loyal clients and premium services.

Action Steps

- List the Critical Success Factors for your business.
- Select Key Performance Indicators to measure how well your business is performing compared to expectations.
- Review your current client list, and rank them according to a system that works for you.
- Fire your most problematic client to make room for new services and new clients.

Conclusion

The first thing you need to do if you are serious about building your bookkeeping business is to spend time determining your Critical Success Factors, Key Performance Indicators, and a profile of your ideal client. Without these components, you really do not have the necessary tools to determine whether you are growing in the right direction. We have had an interesting journey as we discovered the importance of applying the 8 Pillars for Exponential Business Growth to your bookkeeping business in order to ensure maximum capacity for growth going forward.

The 8 Pillars for Exponential Business Growth offer us ways to save time in our busy lives and to grow with purpose. Look for creative ways to implement changes to each Pillar, and watch what can happen to your business.

Appendices

Appendix 1: Bookkeeping Business Assessment Tool

Rate yourself on the following points on a scale where minus five represents strong disagreement with the statement, zero represents complete neutrality, and positive five represents strong agreement. Once you have ranked how your business currently aligns with the questions, tally your score. A negative or low score is indicative of problems or areas for improvement. The closer your score is to one hundred, the more likely you are to have a firm that is rewarding personally and professionally.

1. We have a compelling vision that guides our actions in all that we do.
2. We have leaders who inspire people through their actions, and they provide clear examples through their actions.
3. Team members are encouraged to actively participate and to add value to client relationships.
4. Our firm atmosphere fosters open communication in support of the firm's vision.
5. Our firm adds value to all of our clients through all of our service offerings.
6. Our firm is focused on helping clients increase their profits, increase the value of their business, and address their business challenges.
7. We regularly create room for conversations with clients to learn about their needs.
8. We provide ongoing training and skills development to encourage professional development of our team members.

9. We consciously develop mutually beneficial relationships with our clients in order to understand their needs and our role in meeting those needs.
10. Clients frequently rave about our services and refer their friends to us.
11. Our firm receives value-based fees with strong client retention rates.
12. We frequently seek feedback from our clients as to how we can increase client satisfaction and retention.
13. Our firm experiences an abundance of opportunities from a variety of sources.
14. We are selective in our client acceptance process, focusing only on clients who are aligned with our values and our direction of growth,
15. We continuously seek training opportunities to improve the sales and communications skills of our team members.
16. We have an effective marketing plan that consistently utilizes our marketing collateral, including our website and social media.
17. Our firm leverages cutting-edge technology to effectively and efficiently deliver value added services to our clients.
18. Our firm actively cultivates online resources and cloud solutions to help business clients identify and solve business problems.
19. Our firm has strategic partnerships with other service and product providers that enable us to serve our clients' broader needs.
20. Our firm leverages technology internally to increase effectiveness and efficiency.

Appendix 2: Leveraging the Cloud

The following are just a few suggestions of specific technology or tools that you can readily leverage in order to boost the gains that you will see in each of the 8 Pillars.

Pillar 1: Operational Efficiency

- Reduce overhead—use Google Apps and Box.com to replace traditional e-mail server and client portal.
- Manage work flow—ProWorkflow or Asana to track projects.
- Internal training—BB FlashBack, YouTube, and XMind; record training videos and post on YouTube. Use XMind to document processes and flow.
- Communication—MailChimp and SaneBox to communicate with clients and reduce inbound spam.
- Documentation—DocuSign will help you to track documents requiring signatures, replacing physical documents with electronic documents.
- Scheduling—SimplyBook installed on your website to allow clients to book meetings in time slots that you specify.

Pillar 2: Marketing and Networking

- Seminars—Eventbrite or Meetup for scheduling, marketing, and booking events.
- Webinars—GoToWebinar or AnyMeeting to host online training events for clients and prospects. Use these to document the most common questions that your clients ask. If you repeat

the same answers, you can save some time by presenting them in a group setting.
- Social media—Twitter, LinkedIn, and Facebook are all good places to connect on a deeper level with your clients. LinkedIn is a great tool to research prospects and build a niche.
- Marketing—SendPepper or MailChimp to track outbound e-mail campaigns.
- Sales tracking—Zoho CRM to track activities and contacts. We use Zoho CRM for our marketing side. Once prospects become clients, we transfer them to our client database and mark the lead as closed.

Pillar 3: Sales

- Educating clients—Audacity, BB FlashBack, YouTube
- Product delivery—e-courier.ca, Box.com, DocuSign
- Research—Google search
- Communication—GoToMeeting, AnyMeeting, ProWorkflow

Pillar 4: Niche Development

- Research—Google search, Zoho CRM
- Documentation—XMind, ProWorkflow
- Presentations—Prezi, Apache OpenOffice

Pillar 5: Value Pricing

- Communication—Skype
- Document management—Box.com
- Legal agreements—DocuSign

Pillar 6: Technology

- Virtual PCs—CloudLinx or Cloud9
- Paperless—Box.com, Google Drive
- Payment processing—Stripe or PayPal

Pillar 7: Value Added Services

- Payroll—Ceridian
- External controller—Zoho Books, Wave, and Xero
- Payment processing—Stripe or PayPal
- Credit and collections—Xero
- Cash-flow analysis—PlanGuru

Pillar 8: Practice Management

- Google Apps
- Box.com
- Asana
- Zoho Projects
- YouTube
- GoToMeeting
- AnyMeeting

Appendix 3: Recommended Reading

The Firm of the Future: A Guide for Accountants, Lawyers, and Other Professional Services, by Paul Dunn and Ronald J. Baker

Professional's Guide to Value Pricing, by Ronald J. Baker

The E-Myth Accountant: Why Most Accounting Practices Don't Work and What to Do About It, by Michael E. Gerber and M. Darren Root

The Lean Startup, by Eric Ries

The World Is Flat, by Thomas Friedman

Endless Referrals, by Bob Burg

Supercharge Your Documentation, by Adrienne Bellehumeur

Appendix 4: 24 Secret Technology Solutions for Business Dominance

The following solutions will help you take your business to the next level. This list is not meant to be all-inclusive or detailed, just an introduction to help you start your own research for solutions tailored to your business. The solutions are not listed in any specific order.

Solution	Website	Description
Google Canada	www.google.ca	We usually take Google as a given, but we have a lot of contacts who somehow function without Google as one of their search engines.
SimplyBook	http://simplybook.me	Free and easy online reservation tool, allowing your customers to book times that work for both parties without the back and forth.
Google Chrome	https://www.google.com/chrome/browser	A fast, free, lightweight browser that lets you use a profile to synchronize browser favorites and history across multiple devices.
Zoho CRM	https://www.zoho.com/crm	Customer Relationship Management tool to track prospects, opportunities, and clients all in one place.
Zoho Books	https://www.zoho.com/books/pricing	Online accounting software that integrates with Zoho CRM.

Google Apps for Business	http://www.google.ca/enterprise/apps/business	E-mail, calendar, and online cloud storage are just the start— see what else the Google Apps Marketplace has for your business.
BB FlashBack	http://www.bbsoftware.co.uk/bbflashback.aspx	A screen recorder to capture video and audio. Use this as a tool for staff training videos and external communication. They also have a free version, called BB FlashBack Express.
Audacity	http://audacity.sourceforge.net	Free, open-source, cross-platform software for recording and editing sounds. We use it to record and edit podcasts for clients.
Xero	http://www.xero.com	Online accounting software suitable for businesses from a simple start-up to complex.
Wave	https://www.waveapps.com	Small business accounting software, specifically targeted toward businesses with fewer than ten employees. Includes payroll options and payment processing.
ProWorkflow	http://www.proworkflow.com	Manage projects online; include your team and your clients as collaborators.
Asana	https://asana.com	Teamwork without e-mail; tool to encourage collaboration and track tasks.

Expensify	https://www.expensify.com	Digital expense reporting that works.
MailChimp	http://eepurl.com/WEL-v	Create e-mail newsletters and campaigns to communicate with your clients.
Box	www.box.com	Simple, secure file sharing from anywhere. I use this as an alternative to a portal.
XMind	http://www.xmind.net	I use mind mapping to help with collaboration—this is a great tool to visually demonstrate project requirements and work flow.
Apache OpenOffice	https://www.openoffice.org	A free and open productivity suite that provides a free alternative to Microsoft Office.
SendPepper	http://sendpepper.com?ref=475339	E-mail marketing and automation software for small business.
SaneBox	http://sanebox.com/t/o5qos	Sort and categorize e-mail; eliminate spam and reduce unimportant e-mails.
Skype	http://www.skype.com/en	Videoconferencing, instant messaging, and voice calls all in one place.

YouTube	https://www.youtube.com	We use YouTube channels to share videos, either internally with staff or externally with clients and prospects.
e-courier	http://www.e-courier.ca	Safe and secure means to transmit large files; very similar to e-mail but without the security issues and file size limits.
DocuSign	https://www.docusign.com	Capture the power of the Internet for modern business; this tool provides electronic signatures for all documents.
AnyMeeting	http://www.anymeeting.com	Web conferencing for small business, offering a free solution as well as paid solutions.

This list was compiled by Dream Practice, a group of like-minded business advisors working to enhance the bookkeeping and accounting businesses that we have the privilege of serving. You can learn more about us at www.dreampractice.ca.

Appendix 5: Niche-Development Example

We will go through the necessary steps in order to build a niche focused on dentists. For greater clarity, we will focus on dentists in the Calgary area. We can draw a more detailed picture, but this outline gives us enough information to start. We are using Google search for this exercise; your results may differ if you use a different search engine. Likewise, you may receive different results as time passes—the Internet is extremely fluid.

Keep in mind that this is a long-term process; if you are building a niche, we assume that you are looking for long-term growth. The time you invest in the development stage will yield significant results going forward.

Typically, I see dental students graduating and going out on their own. For the first two or three years they do everything themselves to save money. At some stage, they either realize that they are in over their heads or they are too busy to handle the paperwork. You can either wait for them to reach out to you at the pain stage, or you can approach them and offer business start-up sessions for students who are about to graduate. Personally, I prefer the proactive approach because the students will follow your advice and will seek you out once they are ready. The first time leaves you with a two- or three-year lag, as you have to wait until they graduate and are ready for you. The dental colleges will literally be producing a new batch of clients for you every year. After two or three years, you will have a steady flow of new and ambitious clients. The real upside is that you have already trained them, so they will follow your advice and will be extremely loyal—they are too busy to look for a new bookkeeper or accountant.

For our example, we will identify resources and comment on how they could be leveraged; we will not go beyond the initial level of research.

Step 1: Ideal Client

We specifically selected dentists in the Calgary area. This description will be specific enough for our purposes. If you really want to specialize, you could break this down further by dental specialties or practice size.

Step 2: Training

The next step is to determine how or where these individuals are trained. Our Google search for "dental schools calgary" yielded 128,000 results. Most will be irrelevant, but we do see that the University of Alberta in Edmonton has a "Calgary Dental General Practice Residency" program offering. That is a good start to our research. Make note of any industry relationships or department heads at this stage—you can research them further to see if they have any significant speaking engagements or are published in any publications.

Step 3: Professional Associations

Searching next for "dental association Calgary," we receive 303,000 results. From here, we learn that the following are relevant:

- Calgary and District Dental Society (CDDS)—http://cdds.ca

- Alberta Dental Association and College—http://www.abda.ab.ca
- Canadian Dental Association—http://www.cda-adc.ca/en/oral_health/index.asp
- Academy of General Dentistry—http://www.agd.org
- OSAP.org—http://www.osap.org

These are all very interesting sites. If you visit them, you will see that a lot of them indicate industry partners or event sponsors. We will use these contacts when we research suppliers to the dental industry.

The Canadian Dental Association (http://www.cda-adc.ca/en/about/nlda) is a great resource. It actually provides details about their national conference, including a description of the events and speakers. These will all be subject to further research. The Canadian Dental Association site also refers us to the Alberta Dental Association and College. Again, the speakers and sponsors for the conference will be potential channel partners for you over time.

Step 4: Develop Channel Partners and Referral Sources

The Canadian Dental Association National Conference lists their vendors on their site: http://www.nlda.net/tradeshowcda.html. Use Google to learn more and identify the contact details for the speakers and sponsors. Once you know your audience, reach out to them to learn what you can about the industry, especially areas of concern and emerging or new solutions. Focus on the areas that you can use to differentiate your services; don't try to compete against established traditional bookkeepers. Your true growth opportunities lie in the marginal areas where few have thought to go.

Step 5: Social Media

This is a broad category, but we will restrict our social media research solely to LinkedIn. The other platforms are beneficial as well, but you can see the value if we focus just on LinkedIn. Search Google for "dental group linkedin." There are roughly 4.5 million results. You can use your research thus far to narrow it down, or you can start general. Join the relevant groups and monitor them to see who is commenting and what the conversations look like. In particular, you are interested in business issues that dentists face. Once you are comfortable, start adding your own comments to the conversation. Ultimately, you want to start your own dental group so that you can control the conversation and be seen as the industry thought leader.

If you want amazing results, determine which social media channels your niche uses and focus on those areas first.

Step 6: Take Action

Now that you have done some preliminary research, find out what information you can add to the conversation. Use LinkedIn to connect with other members of your group. Create a website that includes a reference point for dentists—build a platform that they will visit often. This setup increases your credibility and offers some insight into your process. If you are comfortable at this stage, find out what software most dentists are using and do demonstration videos on YouTube to attract more search results.

Step 7: Study Niche-Specific Software

I find that most software companies are looking for ways to connect with their client base and build rapport to generate new sales. If you research the industry for specific solutions, you can reach out to the software vendors and offer to share your webinars or seminars with their audience. I normally recommend doing the events for free in exchange for promotional efforts.

Step 8: Lead Sources

Create a list of your lead sources, and input them into your CRM. Now that you have a solid lead database, put your research into action by reaching out to them. If you have done your homework thus far, you actually have enough knowledge to put together a course or webinar for your audience.

Step 9: Offer Training Courses

Use your research from the previous steps in order to learn what you can about the unique features of your niche as an industry. Put these materials together, and offer them as either live seminars or webinars for your clients and prospects. This is a great growth opportunity once you have a few clients in your niche, as they will bring friends and colleagues to your presentations.

Step 10: Create Value Added Services

Based on your research, you should now be fairly comfortable with the needs of your niche group. Specifically, you want to identify the issues that they struggle with and offer solutions tailored to their needs—solve business problems with technology solutions, help with implementation, etc.

Step 11: Charge Accordingly

As you build your perceived value and your technical skills, you can start to increase your fees. Build your niche into a profitable area in your business.

Step 12: Cull Clients That Are Not within Your Niche

Find other bookkeepers that are interested in the clients you may no longer wish to service. You can usually sell a block of clients or simply assist them with transition. Either way, you are helping them find someone who can focus on them. As a growth tool, you can leverage this by finding other niche-conscious bookkeepers and transition relevant clients to them. In turn, they will keep you in mind if they encounter prospects that fit within your niche.

Appendix 6: Business Growth Experiment

We are conducting a bookkeeping experiment to prove that cloud technology works. We choose bookkeeping over a full accounting firm because there are fewer moving parts to monitor—we can control the variables easily and maintain a scalable operation without interference from the deadlines and complexities of accounting and tax. We will prove that commodity work like data entry can provide a scalable and viable revenue stream for any accounting firm. Once we have the systems and processes working smoothly, we will work with accountants to expand our experiment to their firms.

Challenge:

- Build an effective, scalable, efficient business using technology.
- Embrace cloud solutions to improve efficiency.
- Build stronger client relationships.
- Leverage the 8 Pillars to generate exponential and sustainable growth.

We chose cloud solutions that would allow us to create a scalable model with flexibility. We anticipate low overhead, high responsiveness, and quick turnaround. We will leverage technology in order to build strong relationships within a virtual team and among our clients.

As part of our experiment, we have identified several options in each area and will document our choices and decisions. We plan to truly document the best practices at www.bookkeepingbusinessexperiment.com.

About the Author

Jeff Borschowa had his first consulting gig at the age of ten years old. Jeff's fifth-grade class bought a Commodore 64 to be used as a communal resource. Jeff had experience with the Commodore 64, so he was appointed as the official classroom trainer. A lifelong passion was ignited, and Jeff has been an avid fan of technology since then.

Jeff majored in accounting at the University of Alberta but still took many electives in the technology field. Jeff's experience with technology carried forward into his subsequent career, and he was often brought in as a troubleshooter to resolve issues.

In his career, Jeff learned that a lot of the challenges faced by small-business owners, including bookkeepers and accountants, were caused by using outdated or inadequate technology. We have all seen significant advances in cloud technology, and Jeff has dedicated his efforts to finding the best of the best and truly building dream practices for his clients.

Jeff is an entrepreneur first and a business advisor second—he brings his experience and practical solutions to every client situation that he encounters.

Jeff lives in Calgary, Alberta, Canada, with his wife and two wonderfully rambunctious boys.

About the Book

Running your own bookkeeping business can be both rewarding and challenging at the same time. Often, bookkeepers are busy working in their businesses and forget to focus on the big-picture areas that ensure growth and sustainability.

In the 8 *Pillars for Exponential Business Growth*, Jeff Borschowa discusses the key obstacles that bookkeepers face and provides practical solutions to take your business to the next level.

Established and start-up bookkeepers will both benefit from the materials in this book. The book focuses on critical technology and work-flow solutions that can streamline your business. Once operations are firmly in hand, the next step is to scale the business up through significant growth. Ideas and tools are offered to get you well on your path to exponential growth.

www.ingramcontent.com/pod-product-compliance
Lightning Source LLC
Chambersburg PA
CBHW021949200526
45163CB00018B/1443